YOUR COMPLETE LIBRA 2022 PERSONAL HOROSCOPE

Monthly Astrological Prediction Forecasts of Zodiac Astrology Sun Star Sign- Love, Romance, Money, Finances, Career, Health, Spirituality

Iris Quinn

Contents

PERSONALITY PROFILE

Constellation: Libra

Zodiac symbol: Balance Scales

Date: September 22 – October 22

Zodiac element: Air

Zodiac quality: Cardinal

Greatest Compatibility: Sagittarius and Aries

Sign ruler: Venus

Day: Friday

Color: Green and Pink

Birthstone: Opal

Libra is represented by scales. Librans have a forgiving spirit; when you offend them and ask for their forgiveness, you are sure to be forgiven by Libras quickly. They are relationship-focused and usually don't let go of their relationship easily, even when all is not going well. They are fair in judgment.

Libras are good negotiators, and they don't just buy a good or idea anyhow, so you hardly win them in negotiations. They are considerate when making decisions. Also, they are easily laid back and social butterflies. They can also be flirtatious and easily misunderstood because of their nature.

They are superficial and overly agreeable. If a Libra wants to avoid disagreement, they agree to everything even when they truly disagree. They can also be unpredictable and so indecisive; decision making is a big problem for Libras. They are passive-aggressive and lazy.

Venus

Venus rules Libra and the second house, further symbolizing love, beauty, romance, relationships, finances, luxury, creativity and sensuality- pleasure and earthly pleasurable pursuits. Venus is sometimes seen as a Goddess, the Goddess of love, beauty & sexuality, and this shows what we can take from Venus.

This planet's influence is feminine, yet despite bringing the divine feminine into our lives Venus also represents materialism; money, finances and resources. Pleasure is rooted in the physical and material realm so this is how Venus influences us, the worth and value you give possessions comes under Venus's realm.

Self-worth and self-esteem are associated here too. Unique soul gifts and talents, charm and charisma can be acquired and strengthened with Venus. The way you see yourself in terms of attractiveness... scent, smells, pheromones, the energy exchanges you feel and desire, and virtually everything related to love, romance and platonic intimacy as well as sexual needs, urges and experiences are included. Security is another major theme.

Venus symbolizes depth, authenticity and transparency- the bonds and loving feelings we experience that are rooted in rawness and vulnerability and not superficiality. The lower vibration of Venus, Venus' shadow, manifests as a lack or absence of self-love; issues in worthiness, the ability and willingness to manifest abundance and money, and create harmonious, loving and mutually respectful and affectionate partnerships are themes. Furthermore, Venus rules our sentiments and sensual urges and instincts. How we approach love, our values and ideals in romance and partnerships, inner beauty and external beauty, how we beautify ourselves, and our charm and social grace. Artistic inclinations and what we find visually pleasing come under Venus' reign- the type of music, art, exercise and movement choices, and inspiration you seek.

Month by Month Forecast

January 2022

Horoscope

Libra will be full of desires and ambitions to succeed in life. This January, you will be taking risks, and with fateful steps, you will get to perform your plans successfully. Enjoy this month as a new beginning, a kick-start in your adventures in life.

You may expect possible level-up in your relationships. You will probably get engaged, or married couples may enjoy a new house this year. There is a lot of exciting milestones for you, Libra. Always be grateful to God and remain faithful to Him, and He will help ease your burdens in life.

Love and Romance

A romantic breeze will envelop your love nest this month. It connotes an impending proposal, engagement, or pregnancy. Somehow it will open you into a new perspective or adulting stage.

You will experience genuine happiness and bliss as a parent to your newborn. Educate yourself and learn as much as you can so you can take care of your budding family early on.

Single Libra will have the chance to find their one great love. Passionate love and intimacy will surround Librans this January. The incoming year brings joy and excitement despite the pandemic.

Work and Career

Be happy with your love life, and do not be affected by what is happening in your career. It does not mean you are unfateful this month. The bad news in your work will not entirely represent what your life will be. The issues in your projects must stay at work, and your social life will remain positive.

You may meet a controlling boss, and employment rules may appear strict to you. Even if you struggle, hold on and maintain your composure. Your seniors will appreciate you, and the company will value you even more.

Money and Finances

With your current financial status, you will have the ability to meet your necessary expenses on time. Expect some form of reward or bonus as a fruit of your diligence and perseverance.

Your career will help you yield better income, so make sure that you are continuously improving yourself. With your enthusiasm, you can become a better person, and it will pave the way to have a slush fund for emergencies.

Earning a living is quite difficult for everyone during the pandemic, so brace yourself and try to keep your job. With creative ideas and business concepts or ventures, you will have a chance to create more sources of revenue.

Health and Spirituality

Prioritize your health and commit to your fitness goals. A slow start is still a step towards getting better, so stick to it, and it will be easier for you to make yourself healthier.

A leaner physique requires an effective diet plan. Your psychological well-being will also be better when you gradually transform your lifestyle into a sustainable and healthier routine.

Changing your habits may also bring changes to your spiritual connection. A positive environment will be great for meditation and imagination. Pray and ask God for help in times of trouble, and you will reach your goals with comfort and ease.

February 2022

Horoscope

Even if you are unwilling, something must come to an end. This month can be a period of stagnation for you, Libra. You may be clinging to something that's already gone.

Try to overcome your hatred to dealing with pain and loss because it binds you to memories and prevents you from moving on.

Love and Romance

You'll most likely cling to a relationship that has already soured. Either because you still love each other after such a long time together, or because you are afraid of being alone.

Your decision as a couple will determine how well your relationship can withstand everyday problems. You will survive the trials if you are both willing to allow each other to make things happen and if you want to grow together.

Your love life issues are minor, but you may go through serious discussions to resolve them. Yes, you must have a genuine desire to find a solution. If you don't know how to adjust, then your relationship may end. Single Libras honor humility., so make an effort not to be overconfident.

Work and Career

Job losses are likely to put you in a tight financial situation. February is associated with loss or the end of something, but it can also relate to physical death.

Someone on your team may be going through a particularly trying time in his life. You may have to shoulder his burden to finish a project.

If you are currently employed, your financial situation may force you to resign or face an untimely dismissal. Isn't that harsh? But, whether you like it or not, there will be subtle changes.

Money and Finances

It denotes the end of an era and the beginning of a new career path. In terms of finances, expect your sources to deteriorate. So, you must learn to bend and purchase just what you need.

Being alive requires survival instinct. In a civilized world like ours, it does not only mean learning how to feed yourself in the period of scarcity but having savings to stretch during emergencies and lockdown.

Health and Spirituality

Make an effort not to conceal information about your physical condition. Discover your body and watch for any changes you've undergone. Try to engage in stress management because pressure and anxiety can also adversely affect your health.

Your fitness is essential. But you have to look after your psychological and emotional health more than anything else. It should be your priority since
certain life-long events can cause us to lose our sanity.

March 2022

Horoscope

You have a tendency to rationalize your actions, defend yourself, and shift blame to others. Avoid doing these things if you don't want to be caught off guard with negative outcomes. This month will demand you to accept responsibility for your actions and to rely on facts rather than making excuses for your shortcomings.

Go out of your comfort zone and look for the possibilities of life. You can do more in life if you can persuade yourself that you can be better. You have tremendous potential, and with so many opportunities available to you in this world, you can achieve far more than you are currently enjoying.

Love and Romance

Legal proceedings may spell the end of your love tale. This month, your love life will be unsatisfying because things may shift and turn turtle between you and your partner. If you're in a relationship with an abusive individual, address your difficulties immediately and try to change or leave the relationship before the problem worsens.

Simple things can provide you delight, and one of these is your independence. Although being free and away from your lover's touch and embraces is not your ideal situation, it will be for the better. So, please be patient while things unfold. It is always prudent to prioritize your protection.

Work and Career

You will be in charge of your own planet. Do not allow others to dominate you or limit your potential. This August, you may feel stuck at work and that your supervisors don't appreciate your efforts.

It is not the greatest moment for you to sit back and relax so that you have complete control over your life, and when people do not appreciate your work and you are not acknowledged in the way that you deserve, muster the confidence to go. Find a place where you can grow and where your abilities will be valuable.

Money and Finances

Your financial resources are identical, and your job pays you at the same rate. Earn as much as you can spend. Remember that in order for things to change, you must do something new. If you want to make more money, you must think of better ways to make more money.

You have a better chance of achieving financial success. Leaving your previous work or career may lead to a more profitable opportunity.

Although money is not your primary motivation for traveling, your hunt for a better firm will result in unanticipated financial gain. It will allow you to save a lot of money for yourself and your family.

Health and Spirituality

It's a time for rest and relaxation. Your capacity to see things in a lighthearted manner will reduce your worry and despair. Remember that issues may be resolved; else, why bother? If you believe there isn't any, why bother thinking? Aside from that, keep your cool and never consider taking your life. If you resist negativity in all your transactions, you will be able to overcome anything life throws at you.

March will usher you into your power. You will discover the path that spiritually enriches you, and this will be your source of inspiration. Your freedom will enable you to get intimately active in spiritual upliftment.

April 2022

Horoscope

The month of April indicates that you will be productive, but be cautious because this may be at the cost of someone else or as a result of someone else's generosity. It denotes that you will be generous; you will make unrestricted gifts and share without any hidden intentions. You will not resort to phony charity to gain people's attention.

Even if you are through a financial drought, the people around you will assist you. The offer of aid should also serve as a caution because someone in authority may wish to help you, but they may do so in exchange for anything in return. Keep an eye out and attempt to determine if it is genuine kindness; otherwise, avoid them.

Love and Romance

Try not to get duped. Even if you are having a difficult time, ensure that your financial situation does not influence your actions. Consider your options, and remember that someone in need may misinterpret politics as a sort of charity. Your trusting heart may lead you astray, leaving you exposed.

Lies can be so powerful that they blind us to what is true. So, above all, learn to look into your partner's heart. Instead of looking at the price, consider whether it comes with love.

If you are in a relationship, you will be content, happy, and comfortable. Your commitment will be more substantial, and I will attend to your emotional, mental, and physical demands.

Work and Career

Professionally, the possibility of obtaining a specialty exists. Success is unavoidable, but it will not be simple, and you may require a few drops of pain reliever. You may have to go through some difficult moments. This month is ideal for employment and career advancement.

You're likely aiming for professional success or advancement. If you are merely looking for work, this could refer to employment and a pleasant working environment.

Perhaps you will also find a friend in your supervisor or an influential individual associated with your firm who will provide advice, time, and support. You will advance in your career, and your financial situation will improve.

Money and Finances

This month indicates that you will most likely remain unemployed. You could potentially lose a promotion, be fired, or be undervalued at work.

It could be a phase of regret since you should have been nice to others as you ascended. Know that you will run into them again when you slide down the success ladder. So, if you were not as pleasant as you should have been, you should accept your mistakes.

Be fair and considerate to everyone you work with, whether they are subordinates or bosses. However, be cautious while taking assistance because their act of compassion may be conditional.

Health and Spirituality

This period may indicate that your vitality will considerably improve. Focus on your health and seek treatment for the complex ailment you are dealing with. Although there may be a delay in seeking medical advice or the possibility of receiving an incorrect diagnosis, you will receive the necessary therapy.

Be modest and use the medical choices that are offered to you. This month will be an excellent opportunity to share your spiritual understanding and faith. You will be generous in sharing your spiritual insights and your spiritual path.

You will be charitable enough to generously increase other people's learnings by revealing your life blunders, which can be embarrassing and prejudicial.

May 2022

Horoscope

Libra will be dealing with hearts in May. For couples, this could indicate that you are about to tie the knot. It is a message of hope for lovers.

This month will be hectic for you because a lot will happen in your relationship. In business, it has a corresponding meaning. This month, you and someone you trust will form a partnership.

You will not be concerned about your health since you will hear positive news about your health. There will be many difficulties in the area of financial, but you will be able to manage this on your own. However, after you and your sweetheart reconcile, you may achieve stability. There will be a flood of good fortune and blessings.

Love and Romance

Single Libras will be influenced by sexual impulses and need physical attraction. Strong and sensible, yet when it comes to love, your emotions will take control. There's a good chance you'll start a new relationship this month, and your love will be contagious enough to make others envious.

Dates and playful nights will be enjoyed by couples. There will be thrilling occasions in your relationship that will strengthen your bond.

Genuine happiness and contentment will exude from you, and you will both provide encouragement, love, support, and respect for one another.

Work and Career

Someone at work will be flirting with you, which can be advantageous because he or she is eager to bear your weight just so you will notice them. If you are already devoted to someone, be careful not to send the incorrect signals, as this can lead to something harmful. It may have an impact on your relationship with your sweetheart in the long run.

You will do well at work. This month isn't going to be particularly exciting. You will be able to balance family and work because you will be working in a happy setting.

This month, unemployed Libras should expect to find work. Although your job will not be in a high-level position, it will give you with enough money to meet your family's basic necessities.

Money and Finances

When it comes to money, you'll have enough to handle your living expenditures at home. You can even afford to own and care for a pet. You are, however, a long way from being able to live comfortably in a large house with your own automobile.

You will have a strong desire to invest and do business. There is a chance that you may form an efficient business collaboration with a possible partner, and your realistic goals will assist both of you in realizing your company dreams.

During the pandemic, young Libra will have the opportunity to be financially secure. Libra will be able to earn money online because to the high demand for internet contributors.

Health and Spirituality

When it comes to health, Libra is in for some good news. Libra women may have increased libido, which could lead to pregnancy. You are in good health, but you must be cautious of the effects of sweets on your body. You have a high risk of having diabetes, which can lead to a variety of health problems.

You have a deep connection with the spiritual realm, and the universe is sending you messages to assist you. This month may bring you a lot of happiness and blessings. It denotes that your intellect, soul, and body are all working together to discover and follow the route that leads to Him.

Horoscope

Libra, you must believe that you are not always to blame for everything. Sacrificial? Selfless? Or is it stupidity? Logic dictates that you may have been at fault for something at some point, but blaming yourself all the time is ludicrous.

Pay attention to your conscience. When you feel guilty about anything, it is possible that you are at blame. As a result, you must accept responsibility for your acts as well as the immediate repercussions.

However, do not accept responsibility for things beyond your control, even if you were the last straw. You have a tendency to overthink, which has a negative impact on your psychological well-being. The month of June conjures up images of balance, serenity, and impartial justice.

Love and Romance

Your relationship's strength is dependent on you as a couple. Regardless of what you have to offer or the mistakes you make, it is necessary for both of you to act and survive and for your inactions to fade away. Your partnership is likely to suffer from some imbalance as a result of secrecy and misconduct. Prepare to be revealed if you are currently doing something wrong against your lover.

This month could be the month when your secrets are revealed. So, if you care about your partner and your relationship, accept your errors and do the right thing.

Deception has the potential to undermine trust, which in turn has the potential to kill love. Stay away from temptations and commit if you are content to be with the one you are with.

Work and Career

Opportunities will undoubtedly present themselves to you. You'll be amazed to see how much money comes in from unexpected places. This month, however, you must only engage in lawful types of job or business.

Always have a balance between your professional and personal lives. It can be tempting to concentrate more on your career because of a higher salary or prospects for growth. Money may shift your priorities in life, but ask yourself why you need the money in the first place. If you respond in the affirmative, you already know what should be your top priority.

Money and Finances

This month, your money will grow almost imperceptibly. Use your earnings to accomplish good and stay away from vices.

Gambling, theft, and other unethical and illegal activities can devastate your financial stability. Take caution when incurring investment risks. Defrauding individuals may provide you with additional income, but your firm may suffer as a result of the fact that you are using the proceeds of a crime as additional capital. Stealing money, no matter how much, is wrong.

Health and Spirituality

Balance must be maintained for greater health by eating, exercising, and relaxing in moderation. Too much of anything can cause a life imbalance.

Avoid overworking because it might lead to weariness. Obesity is caused by overindulging in food. Drinking liquor in moderation can raise your level of intoxication. Maintaining a healthy balance by doing things in moderation is the key to good health.

July 2022

Horoscope

For Libra, the month of July brings ideas of abundance, happiness, wealth, and a fresh start. You will live a life that is proactive.

It's possible that you'll be able to make your desires come true as a result of this. You are enthusiastic and optimistic about your future, and you believe that everything will go well in all aspects of your life, including your profession and personal life.

Love and Romance

In issues of the heart, you will have a fresh start. You'll come across someone who makes you feel protected and secure. You'll be able to devote more time to enhancing yourself and your relationship with each other. In general, you appear to be in a good place because you are both capable of living alone.

If you're single, this could signal that you've had opportunities for love but haven't pursued them. Perhaps you were harmed in a past relationship and are now experiencing trust and security concerns as a result.

Your current weakness and anxiousness will prevent you from trusting new lovers. As a result, take your time getting to know your possible spouse before committing to a relationship. Couples, on the other hand, are likely to feel insecure and unstable in their commitment. Selfishness, greed, and envy are likely to be among the challenges you'll face.

Work and Career

Your profession will also undergo abrupt adjustments, the most of which will be for the better. It's possible that you'll get promoted or employed, or that fresh chances will present themselves.

You must consider the prospects at work that may lead to your promotion since if they are overlooked, they may be delayed or altogether thwarted. Job loss, redundancy, or a lower-paying job offer can all be powerful indicators of negativity.

Money and Finances

Your financial situation is also steady, and you will be able to repay your loans or debts as they fall due. These days, money will not be an issue, and you may even be able to share your blessings with others in need. This is a clear indication that you should consider making investments to earn passive income because it is a positive month.

Certain company operations can result in considerable financial losses. Your savings will be extremely beneficial to you. As a result, make sure to tighten your belt from time to time.

Health and Spirituality

This month has the potential to offer wonderful news. If you are currently ill, this indicates that you will recover quickly. Your health will improve as you adjust your eating habits, and you will totally recover with enough activity.

In the context of spirituality, you might want to try out new techniques or practices to help you calm down. For you to handle your spiritual side, try to find solace in places of worship and discuss other people's perspectives on their beliefs. It is always simpler to learn about the Lord's gospels when they are shared with others.

Horoscope

Libra will take on a more youthful attitude. You'll be a little playful and outgoing, and you'll meet someone with whom you can have private chats.

This month, you'll be inundated with fantastic news. Perhaps you will no longer be concerned with worldly issues since you enjoy life with all of its ups and downs. This month, you'll take on challenges and show that you're capable of overcoming obstacles.

When it comes to working, you may think it strange, yet you prefer beating the deadline to submitting sooner.

Love and Romance

This August, you're in for a romantic adventure. If you're still young and unmarried, you might be able to form new connections or meet your puppy love.

If you're in a relationship, on the other hand, you'll enjoy the thrill this month brings because your horoscope promises sexual desire and adventure. In its purest form, love will bloom unexpectedly.

Your family relationships will be strengthened as well. You will travel whenever the opportunity arises, and your relatives will be pleased to see you taking advantage of your independence.

Work and Career

In general, you will receive favorable news in terms of your career and finances. You'll begin with a fun career or a new business venture.

You will locate a job that is far superior to your expectations. You may even be required to travel for business, and there is the chance of advancement.

When you are confronted with a dilemma, you will need to act quickly. However, if it impacts the firm, it will be critical that you convey your opinions openly to your superiors before making appropriate selections.

Money and Finances

Your money will be under control as a result of your successful business activities and investments. You must, however, keep an eye on your expenditures because it may lead to bankruptcy. Spend a little money and save a lot of money.

This month, you'll be able to literally put your money to work for you. Investing in stocks or franchising is a terrific way to make money this year. You can also put your imagination to use by taking advantage of virtual activities such as painting, drawing, singing, and much more.

Health and Spirituality

Make an effort to better your general health. Make an effort to break poor habits by scheduling outside activities that you can perform every day and making it a habit to fit these activities into your hectic schedule.

To deepen your spiritual connection, you might wish to try a different path. It suggests that your present organization or religion isn't as effective at motivating you to be faithful as the new one you're investigating.

Your spiritual development is more important than anything else, so be sure you're following someone who talks about God rather than oneself.

September 2022

Horoscope

Libra will possibly feel the influence of Aquarius in all aspects of life, be it in career, relationships, health, or finance this month. September will be calm for most of you, but those born close to Leo will have a different fate, perhaps a little bit luckier.

Expressing your emotion is the key. You will be a bit sentimental this month, but your loved ones will completely understand you.

Love and Romance

Maybe it's not yet time. You have a strong desire to fall in love and a little desperate to be in a relationship.

Single Libra will meet a person with whom they will feel chemistry, and will desire to be committed. Your emotions are strong, so try to make your logic work, or else you might make mistakes over and over.

For those in a relationship, your hunger for physical touches is written all over your face. But don't worry, your partner is a willing prey. However, be cautious about who you are dating, for some people feel uncomfortable when their partners are touchy-feely.

Work and Career

You are likely to be a little bit inefficient when September starts compared to your work performance last month. Your disappointments are unavoidable, but you can still resolve problems at work. Avoid rushing things for you to bounce back and overcome your failures. Do it little by little.

Opportunities for unemployed Libra will open. Your perseverance and the ability to showcase your skills, a lot of industries will be pleased to have you on their team. Your innate creativity will help you become successful and fame if possible, but it will be a challenging path.

For the early months this year, you will give back to your community through donations and volunteer work.

Money and Finances

Hooray! It will be a good year for your business. You will reap the positive results of your hard work. Since you have the enthusiasm to pursue your dreams, your market will appreciate your personal touches, and they will acknowledge the effort you have exerted in the products or services you are offering.

You will be able to witness your business grow in the right direction with your creativity. Business expansion is waving in a few months, be ready.

Be careful in choosing the person that will manage your financial dealings. Your earnings are high, and business opportunities are too many. Choose someone you trust and who will consider confidential matters strictly confidential.

Health and Spirituality

Health is wealth. You can afford the luxurious things in the world, but don't forget that you won't be able to enjoy these things when you are no longer strong and healthy? Remember the value of your life. You may only live once, and we must make the most of it.

Be mindful of what you are eating. Be productive without sacrificing your health. Make a menu of all kinds of food you love and make a healthier version of them.

With all the blessings that go your way, never forget to be grateful and pray. Everything you have, even your very life, is borrowed. In the end, it is not our money that will matter, but the depth of our relationship and faith in our Creator.

October 2022

Horoscope

Libra, this month will be prosperous for you! This October, you will be blessed in a variety of ways. You may receive invitations to vacations, good marks in school, a job advancement, and other pleasant surprises. You will be given material things as well as intangible gifts such as family unity, wisdom, a strong physique, and a loving partner.

Your cheerful demeanor will shine brightly, and you will provide delight to everyone you meet, young and old. It doesn't mean you won't have troubles this month; it only means you'll be able to deal with them with poise, tranquilly, and calm.

Your good fortune may bring you gifts, rewards, and monetary prizes, but you'll love the rush of anticipation as you confidently declare that you'll be the winner. Perhaps you can bring things to life by thinking about them.

You must maintain your strength during times of need and grief. Learn to empathize and understand how others could feel in a similar circumstance. Being overconfident is a flaw, and obtaining what you want the majority of the time can make you feel entitled. It might cause annoyance and despair.

Love and Romance

Who doesn't want to be happy, passionate, and in love? There is nothing more you could wish for with all the blessings that are always flooding into your household.

However, even in the midst of all the good, evil things can emerge. Your partner may have intended to inform you about some problems at home, but because you're always looking for anything positive, critical things can be overlooked. To save you from becoming injured, other individuals may lie and keep things hidden from you.

Encourage openness and honesty. Although it's wonderful to think positively, be prepared for the unexpected. Instead of living in a fantasy world, be prepared to accept reality, with all of its ups and downs.

Work and Career

You'll be successful, and you might even become renowned for doing what you love.

If you're an artist, a masterpiece might sell for three times its original price; if you're a swimmer, you might be able to dive to the deep and collect an old clam with a large pearl. Even if these sounds unusual, everything is possible when things are going your way.

Money and Finances

This month, your financial situation will be unaffected. To you, the role of chance is incredibly inspiring. You can do whatever you want, whenever you want, and however you want because of the gifts you are receiving.

Your blessings also give you power in some way. You should try to maintain your humility and not put your happiness on your financial possessions. When you become extremely competitive and egoistic, you risk becoming self-centered and losing touch with your family.

Health and Spirituality

Be content with what you have and don't obsess over your wealth. It has the ability to make you feel pressed, sacred, and tainted. Keep an eye on your health and your "self." Perhaps you become conceited and full of yourself because you were gifted with the world's goods.

Take time to admire the beauty of nature with your family and enjoy your life and the companionship of others. When everything is said and done, and we reach our spiritual condition, your wealth will be nothing in the eyes of God, and it will be our good deeds that keep us in His grasp.

Horoscope

November is a work month for Libras, so expect extra labor! It will be a month of opportunity and growth. However, as a creature that thrives on hard effort and discipline, you are prone to burnout.

You should remember to look after yourself and your mental health when you take on new tasks. To avoid stress, get assistance if necessary.

And you must have a positive mentality to end the year with a bang and happiness. You've done a fantastic job thus far, and you can go much better.

Love and Romance

Your romantic life will be peaceful, romantic, and harmonious.

51

Your relationship could take a step forward this month. Expect your lover to become more dependent on you in the future. Make every effort to assist, but don't allow your spouse to take advantage of you.

When you have a disagreement, talk to your partner about it. Some of your buddies may exacerbate your situation, so be cautious.

People around you will be more ready to pay attention to you if you are a single person. New friendships are on their way to you. Although questions and what-ifs will always be there in your mind, you may form love relationships with the pals you made this year.

Work and Career

This month, you'll have more opportunities to do what you enjoy – work. You will most likely be busier at work as you will be expected to take on extra chores and responsibilities.

You are a workaholic by nature, but you may feel overwhelmed and fatigued this month as your to-do list grows. But don't worry, your colleagues will come to your rescue.

Don't be frightened to seek assistance. Teamwork is the key to overcoming difficult circumstances at work. Assign and distribute responsibilities to other members of the team.

November is also a favorable month for Libras looking for work. Some job positions demand someone like you, and they are eager to make you a competitive offer with excellent benefits.

Money and Finances

For Libras, this year promises a bountiful inflow of cash as you invest in real properties. Your money will not come easy. It may require physical and mental energy. It may be exhausting, but it will be worth all your effort.

There are people who wants to discourage you from improving your financial status. Just do not listen to them and continue with what you are planning. Life has a great surprise waiting for you.

Health and Spirituality

Although Libra's health started off a little off this year, it will improve as the year goes on. To keep this up, though, you should spend more time outside and engage in more mental activities to boost your mental health. Despite this, Libra's health will be excellent until the end of the year, and it will continue to improve.

December 2022

Horoscope

Libra, you've got a busy month ahead of you! Your bosses will put your abilities to the test, and the project will consume the most of your time. It will not be easy, but with your zeal and natural talent, you will be able to raise their eyebrows with the outcome.

As a relationship, you will have difficulties, but you will be able to overcome them. December is brimming with love and caring, more than enough for you to always choose each other despite disagreements.

The sky fosters passionate connection, which will embrace you and your lover throughout the month. Even the smallest contact and glances will convey your affection for one another. It won't take a country to inform you that you're madly in love.

Love and Romance

Your heart will be at ease, Libra.

There's a chance you'll make progress in your relationship, have a better understanding, and make more plans together. Couples will notice an increase in libido. Marriage discussions are unavoidable as the desire to be together grows greater with each passing day.

As a single Libra, you can see this as an opportunity to try again with love. You might discover joy in new encounters or renew an old flame. Seduction will be your powerful tool, and your sexual drive will be your weakness.

Work and Career

Being organized will allow you to complete chores relatively quickly. Making a precise to-do list for your daily responsibilities is recommended. Plan ahead of time since it will help you achieve more. You're prone to overworking, so prioritize chores.

Surround yourself with wonderful friends who think similarly to you; you'll pick up a lot of life skills from them, and positive exchanges of experiences will help you prepare as you gently climb the success ladder.

No one can control what happens in life, but if you allow hardships to drag you down, you may find yourself defeated. Your career will need a lot of effort from you, so learn as much as you can and keep working on developing yourself.

Money and Finances

You have excellent commercial and financial investing ideas. Make time to share these with the people you care about. You will receive sound advise on planning and implementation. If you're lucky, you might even acquire some financing to make your ideas a reality. Your entrepreneurial abilities, as well as the influence of the stars, indicate that your investments will be profitable.

Libra is already frugal, but this month you will abandon the "good deals," bringing your year to a close with a complete cessation of impulsive purchasing and only spending on what you need when you need it. The desire to save more and manage your finances better can assist you in achieving financial independence in your early years.

Health and Spirituality

In terms of health, you will notice that when someone takes care of you, your recuperation time is shorter. It is past time for you to look for folks who will not only physically but also morally support you. Our bodies deteriorate as we age, and we require more than just physical aid.

Avoid being pessimistic because it can sometimes magnify our fears over our health difficulties. Put your energies to good use and concentrate on self-healing. When you remain calm, joyful, and comfortable, you can recover more quickly.

You can be disconnected from the universe by overthinking. You tend to lose faith and ask all around you if things don't go your way. Nothing remains here eternally, this is only a phase, and we shall go on too. See things in a good position and nurture your above spiritual connection.

Made in the USA
Las Vegas, NV
16 August 2022